Funny Sh*t Drummers Do

A Fun Look at Life Behind a Drum Set

David Aron

ISBN-13: 978-1-7344091-2-3

Books may be purchased by contacting the publisher:

Whyze Group
2233 S. Overlook Rd.
Cleveland, Ohio, USA 44106
jason@whyzegroup.com

CONTENTS

FUNNY SH*T WE DO
TO PLAY DRUMS BETTER

All beginners learn that a paradiddle is
an important drum rudiment.

And, a flam-para-diddle-diddle is
a form of
medieval torture.

As you learn to play a drum set,
you'll learn about
independence—
four limbs playing
four different rhythms
on four different instruments
at the same time.

…And mastering it
will be more impressive than
learning calculus.

Accept it.

Drummers' feet are
the dumbest parts of our bodies.

Proof…

It takes two months to learn
how to play a double-stroke roll
with our hands.

It takes two *years* to learn how to
play a double bass drum roll
with our feet.

.

Is learning to read music hard?
Nope.

And, it'll be less annoying
to your bandmates
than constantly asking them
what to play.

You're a real drummer
if you can translate:

Tama rode her yamaha
to the meinl at the sabian.
Zildjian used paiste
to mapex his gretsch to his pearl.
Ludwig and DW
ate their pork pie.

Drum sets are loud.
Use musician's ear plugs.

Bonus...

Sell ear plugs to
your neighbors
for a little extra cash.

Be prepared for admirers.

If you're learning to play drums in school,
then you're bound to become
the object of puppy love
(even if you still feel
like a geek.)

In your first garage band,
you'll see why you'll never
play loud enough
for electric guitar players.

(Bring your ear plugs.)

Play well with others.
Be nice. Be humble.

You can always be replaced
by a button on a
drum machine.

FUNNY SH*IT WE DO TO EARN MONEY PLAYING DRUMS

In your first rehearsal
with real professionals,
you'll think,
"I've got this."

…until they pull out
a chart
in 13/8 time.

The math of becoming a pro
made sense before
you had to buy
a $20,000 gig van
to move your $3,500 drum set.

Be prepared for anything
when gigging.
Bring extra sticks, drum keys,
drum heads, underwear
and wrenches.

Just kidding about
the underwear.

Lucky you!
You've got your
first paid gig.

Now, roadie your
eleven-piece drum set
up those six flights of stairs
cowboy!

If the venue already has a drum kit,
then you'll only need to bring
your cymbals, pedals,
sticks and extra stands.

Congratulations.

You're carrying only
50 pounds of gear instead of 100.

After years of
tuning drums,
you'll realize that
there's always one lug
on one drum
that goes
p-i-i-i-ng, boink or thud
no matter how
you tune it.

The chance that your
bass drum pedal
will break during a performance
is directly proportional to…

how soon
your drum solo is.

You'll be feeling great about your sixteenth note grooves until sixteenth note *quintuplets* become trendy.

"More cowbell"
pleases audiences
more than
anything else.

And, you only
have to say it.

Be prepared for encores.
It's easy.

No matter whether
you're performing
jazz, rock or musical theater,
there will always be some joker
at the end of a gig
who shouts,
"Free Bird."

MORE FUNNY SH*T

How do you tell if the stage is level?

The drummer is drooling from
both sides of his mouth.

What do you call a drummer
who breaks up with her boyfriend?

Homeless.

A drummer died and went to heaven.

He was waiting outside the pearly gates when he heard the most incredible fast and furious drumming coming from within.

Immediately he recognized the playing and rushed to ask St. Peter if that was Buddy Rich playing drums inside the gates. St. Peter responded, "No. That's God. He just thinks he's Buddy Rich."

How do you get a drummer off your porch?

Pay him ten bucks for the pizza.

What do you say to a drummer
in a three-piece suit?

"Will the defendant please rise?"

A guy walks into a night club and
asks how late the band plays.

The bartender replies, "Oh, about half a beat
behind the drummer."

What's the difference between a drummer and a savings bond?

One will mature and make money.

What's the first thing a drummer says
when she moves to LA?

"Would you like fries with that, sir?"

What's the difference between an amateur drummer and a professional drummer?

An amateur drummer plays gigs on weekends and has a day job.
A professional drummer plays gigs on weekends and has a wife who has a day job.

Note from the Author

Thank you for reading *Funny Sh*t Drummers Do: A Fun Look at Life Behind a Drum Set*. Whatever occasion you're celebrating, I hope this book has added a few minutes of joy to it!

If you've enjoyed this book, I hope you'll write a review on Amazon or wherever you bought this book. It really helps!

Thanks again, and keep on drumming!

-   David Aron